CRASH
- OR THE LAST 30 MINUTES OF A LIFE

Other Books by Ian Gouge

Novels and Novellas

Tilt - Coverstory books, 2023
Once Significant Others - Coverstory books, 2023
On Parliament Hill - Coverstory books, 2021
A Pattern of Sorts - Coverstory books, 2020
The Opposite of Remembering - Coverstory books, 2020
At Maunston Quay - Coverstory books, 2019
An Infinity of Mirrors - Coverstory books, 2018 (2nd ed.)
The Big Frog Theory - Coverstory books, 2018 (2nd ed.)
Losing Moby Dick and Other Stories - Coverstory books, 2017

Short Stories

An Irregular Piece of Sky - Coverstory books, 2023
Degrees of Separation - Coverstory books, 2018
Secrets & Wisdom - Paperback, 2017

Poetry

Crash - Coverstory books, 2023
not the Sonnets - Coverstory books, 2023
Selected Poems: 1976-2022 - Coverstory books, 2022
The Homelessness of a Child - Coverstory books, 2021
The Myths of Native Trees - Coverstory books, 2020
First-time Visions of Earth from Space - Coverstory books, 2019
After the Rehearsals - Coverstory books, 2018
Punctuations from History - Coverstory books, 2018
Human Archaeology - Paperback, 2017
Collected Poems (1979-2016) - KDP, 2017

Non-Fiction

Shrapnel from a Writing Life - Coverstory books, 2022

IAN GOUGE

CRASH
- OR THE LAST 30 MINUTES OF A LIFE

First published in paperback format by
Coverstory books, 2023

ISBN 978-1-7393569-5-8 (paperback)

Copyright © Ian Gouge 2023

The right of Ian Gouge to be identified as the
author of this work has been asserted by him
in accordance with the Copyright, Designs and
Patents Act 1988.

All characters and events in this publication,
other than those clearly in the public domain,
are fictitious and any resemblance to real
persons, living or dead, is purely coincidental.

The cover image was designed by the author ©
Ian Gouge 2023

All rights reserved.

No part of this publication may be reproduced,
circulated, stored in a system from which it can
be retrieved, or transmitted in any form
without the prior permission in writing of the
publisher.

www.iangouge.com

www.coverstorybooks.com

Crash

- after re-reading T.S.Eliot

I

memory is the pattern of tweed
the old wool-work of warp and weft
stitched inside night-time eyelids
the mottled colours of recall
awaiting you when
eyes still closed
you try to rouse from sleep
and find yourself bound in the weave
the life you've woven for yourself
or life has woven about you

warp and weft
in and out

searching for pattern in the not-cloth
is like scanning an archive
for a familial tartan
something to hang on to
when all's said and done

instinctively knowing last night was

it

the final time you might have been
enchanted

memory is the only weapon
we have against death
remembering proves we're alive
even if
like raking over old coals
the cold clinker of our lives
we do nothing but generate dust
ash to be swept up
swept into a bag
disposed of in the black bin
awaiting Monday's collection

there goes my life
tossed by men in hi-vis
into the back of a grubby yellow truck
warning lights flashing

II

there is only one journey
one filled with multiple beginnings
too many to count

and multiple endings
each deceptive
couched in the cloak of a lie
a tartan cloak
frayed at the edges
letting colour bleed out
in fragile skeins of thread
toward a future
where it might be re-woven

by you

warp and weft
in and out

or bagged and binned

we pretend glimpses of conclusion
pretend we understand

like that car shooting a red light
the skid outside the restaurant
tyre-tracks on the road
lines woven into the story

while inside
at the counter   waiters
wait

waved to our table
they saunter over
flourish a plastic menu

voices of temptation

suggest the dish-of-the-day
as if it were a gem
hewn from rock
by a back-broken miner

pausing for our order
he has no interest in beginnings
or endings
only to avoid rebuke
to ensure the pattern on his waistcoat

is aligned
lines and lies peddled
to keep the punters happy

that night could have been
the last time we were

enchanted

at the foot of the menu
in small print
ghosted on natty paper to chime
with the waiters' waistcoats
usual warnings about allergies
disclaimers about the presence
(or absence)
of nuts
statements on the dangers of

self-consumption

the maître d'
replete with recipes
a taste for the obtuse
has a story he likes to tell

about beginnings
and an apple

don't think about the man
think about the bite
and ask
who is there
to make the apple whole again?

beginnings and endings
woven into the fabric of his words too
words hiding behind
the lids of his eyes
in the warp and weft
of skeins and veins

III

under an immeasurable canvas
an illiterate juggler practices still
the necks of his clubs
worn thin by decades of
throwing
catching

dropping
starting again

ask him
and he'll tell you he's just beginning
to get the hang of it

after all this time

listen closely
and hear him count

sixty-two   *sixty-three*   *sixty-four*

as the heavy clubs
pirouette in the air
slip from one hand to the next
like a cheap trick
you're not supposed to notice
eyes fixed on those above his head
wondering if they're high enough
spinning enough

wondering if he's going to let one fall
when he's going to let one fall

sixty-five   sixty-six   thump

chipped enamel flakes into a pattern
not unlike tweed
(or unlike tweed)
crazed like veins
yet the clubs remain what they have always been
hard and solid and unyielding
even in the light's deception
when spinning in the air

or falling to the floor

IV

soon it will be the time of poppies
knitted to railings
crocheted on lampposts
little balloons of red and black

like signposts
both to the past
and the future

poppies woven into the warp and weft
of time

and next time
if there is a next time
if we can find a way
to make it be the last time
what colours will the poppies be
those of remembrance
multicoloured threads
knit into a kind of tartan
almost regular
precise
but not quite
because that is the nature of wool

to be slack
and imprecise

a different kind of failure

children tug to free the poppies
as if it were a game
like 'trick or treat'
expecting a prize

a sweet
a trip to the circus to watch
what

the acrobats
a lion tamer
or the juggler
struggling to find a rhythm
as if somewhere in his head
he can hear

an antique drum

beating out
as he starts again

sixty-six   sixty-five   sixty-four

and the children cheer
faces rouged by excitement
not understanding his goal
nor the meaning of poppies
only knowing
how pretty they look
sewn into the warp and weft

of the horses' tack
the tartan cloak of the ring master

sixty-three   sixty-two   sixty-one

all they want to see
are the clowns
with their flapping feet
and painted faces
the gaudy checks of over-large jackets
as if laughter has been woven in
woven into their walk
the way they fuss and push

the near collision
with the juggler

sixty   fifty-nine   fifty-eight

while outside
rain begins to batter the tent
and the canvas sags
threateningly

and no-one has the heart
to tell the children
this could be the last time
they are ever

enchanted

the juggler continues
the ancient drum beats on
and from somewhere else
just beyond

the still point

comes a sound
no-one else can hear
no-one else can interpret

fifty-seven fifty-six fifty-five

V

take the tea cup to the pot
or to the jug

milk first! milk first!

you watch the white spoil
make the dirty journey to brown
the tones through which it travels
cower unnameable

when did you learn
that 'builder's tea' was a shade of ochre
darker than tan
more sombre than burgundy
less threatening than peat

make it like that

you once said
as if turning colour to taste
in the fusing of senses
(or confusing them)
rejoicing in overlap

the collusion of allies
habitually bent on keeping to themselves

the knowledge of dead secrets

as if they might be parachuted-in
under cover of darkness
whispering meaningless codewords
directions taken from incomplete maps

what did you say? milk first?

each sense pleads for priority
recognition
having kept its secrets far too long

fifty-four   fifty-three   fifty-two

through the open window
you imagine distant music
emanating from a circus tent in the field
and wonder to which pasture the herd
has been evicted

and when they will be back

and how many of them

beef and horseradish?
I've taken the crusts off
because of your teeth

recognising the big-top tune
you play notes in your head
mesmerised by the wave of
their rise and fall
and want to imagine an orchestra
resplendently dressed
safe under the tent's canvas

but you know it to be only a vinyl recording

what was that, dear?

perhaps the acrobats are practicing
interlocking hands to keep them secure
like putting words together

the weft and the warp

or the lion tamer
is cracking his whip
and realises his heart isn't in it
the same old show

even the lion looks bored

and there is the juggler

fifty-one   fifty   forty-nine

each of them with their dead secrets
knowledge of them
in locking hands
cracking whips
tossing clubs just high enough

then the music stops
leaves them frozen mid-action
the acrobat suspended in mid-air
the lion tamer's whip about to crack
the juggler's clubs about to fall

this   you think   is

the still point

or

the unattended moment

between one thing and the next
the in-betweenness
a thing in its own right

fingers an inch apart
the whip's tip an inch away
the club an inch from its apex

before

yes
milk first   please

VI

so
much later
settled into the too familiar couch
absorbed into its pattern
not unlike tweed
(or unlike tweed)
recall with increasing inaccuracy
the waiter
the voice of temptation
menu items not chosen

why not the steak?

I was tempted by the ribollita

that thing with spices sounded interesting

now
laughter is served up
a side-dish defending
against the vagueness of memory

there is a beat in the struggle to recall

forty-eight   forty-seven   forty-six

something to get used to
with an ending of its own perhaps

*what was it the waiter said
about the bite in the apple?*

was that the waiter?

yes, I think so, dear

it seems so long ago

in the corner of the room
the tall clock
ticks
each tick the end of the previous
or its own beginning

forty-five   forty-four   forty-three

and silence falls   between
settles like unexpected dust
layering all our surfaces

stealing definition
from the patterns
we have woven

in and out

from somewhere
a story resurrects itself
kick-started in the vacuum

do you remember that time…

but either you do not recall
or you are scarred by memory
the warp and weft of it
unsure if
after all this time
it's really something
to hang on to
especially knowing tonight might have been
the last time you were

forty-two   forty-one   forty

and an evening fulfils its purpose
as the container of things past

VII

once
his father nagged him

you can't spend time twice

as he watched him lounging
in the intangible world of the mind

and now
and so much later
the echo returns
almost visible
shimmering as if a mirage
shape and sound just out of reach

knowing the truth of it

the tolling bell

he re-hears those words not as admonishment
but as a plea
chiselled into the fabric of everything
and from its sphinx-like mouth
whispering
in the corners of the room
behind the heavy drapes

you can't spend time twice

in the armchair on which father used to sit
he sees the spectre of a ventriloquist's dummy
frozen in silence
fixed on something only it can see
or hear

thirty-nine   thirty-eight   thirty-seven

a solitary juggler in a moth-eaten tent perhaps
or the metronomic ticking of time
leaking away like
rainwater falling helplessly through a grid
away into the drain-black
and out of sight

and with the water
flow secrets
and history
the wisdom that made his father say

you can't spend time twice

paralysed by partial understanding
old words make him ache
knowing he has used them himself
reprised his father's role
the same plea
passed down to another generation
its knowledge lost in the telling
made meaningless by time
by the warp and weft of things
by the drain-black

thirty-six   thirty-five   thirty-four

remembering is a scratched vinyl disc
replaying itself until the repeated phrase
is all there is

the melody forever lost

VIII

the intrusion of a voice

what was that, Simpson?

when do you know it's autumn, sir?

when the path is strewn with the husks of nuts
broken in their futile fall to concrete
or crushed beneath the heavy-tread of
impatient traffic
when the blend of broken shells and yellowing leaves
pattern puddles glossy with early morning rain

when coat collars go up

when your pace slows just a little
when keeping up gets harder
when breath gets shorter
like the lines of verse
you're able to read
without needing
to pause

for

breath

when longing is greater
when remembering is harder
even then
there's joy to be had

the unattended moment
the still point

listening for

unheard music

imagining the things you might have done
encapsulated in broken nut-shells

the husk of meaning

he writes four phrases on the chalkboard
knowing they are two steps away from
understanding
two steps and perhaps forty years

then

you can't spend time twice

thirty-three   thirty-two   thirty-one

what can they know of autumn
these who have yet to experience the fulness of spring

and does it get cold, sir?

cold

like ice on drainpipes
spittle frozen on pavements
ponds made solid enough for skating
one jumper
(or two jumpers)
thick with warp and weft
that heavy coat your granny bought
(and which you hate)
woolly hats and gloves
dug from chests of drawers

or the blood slowing in your veins
the trace of tartan behind your eyelids
where memory struggles to break through

or is that winter

where autumn is already over
and summer is a remembrance
and spring a myth

thirty   twenty-nine   twenty-eight

not cold
but getting there

IX

she asked

have you seen the water on the lake?

the way sunlight streaks the surface
after a squall
elbowing between clouds

turning white horses to diamond
chasing waves to buffet the land

and now
the wind still up
water kissed by moonlight

do you remember when the park flooded?

an overstatement
for the loss of a strip of land
in another lifetime
submerged beneath murky grey
the diamonds long gone

the innocence of gentle lapping
in and out
weft and warp

as if that were the way of things
to not be there
then be there
then gone

like a juggler's clubs pirouetting in the air

twenty-seven   twenty-six   twenty-five

wasn't it up to seven on the flood-gauge?

footfalls echo in the memory

I didn't mean <u>that</u> year…

rhythm and crescendo
the coming and going of water
thrust first against the fell-sides
then down
falling down
into the waiting lake
as if it was there for that purpose
to gather
to nurture

but it <u>was</u> a bad year

who sees the moment
between flood and not-flood
who marks the first trespass
of water onto path or grass

twenty-four   twenty-three   twenty-two

when one thing turns to another
and pivots
about what

the still point

the unattended moment

for someone must be watching
chained to the warp and weft
the inevitability of pattern
searching the clouds for signs of a break
or the wind for another squall
knowing this might be the last time

to catch the white horses
as they whinny from their fathoms-deep stable
and gallop to the waiting shore

twenty-one   twenty   nineteen

*it was
and old Mr. Loomis lost his caravan*

parked it too close to the fence
just to get a better view

selfish

shellfish?

syllables running on the tide of language
in and out
mistaken for diamonds
in the fret
syllables whinnying like horses
or mules
or asses
(who is there to tell the difference)

Old Mr. Loomis
serve him right

eighteen   seventeen   sixteen

then time takes over
the pied piper of closure

time for bed?

you go, dear
I'll be along directly

as soon as he has stared
at the drain-black water on the lake a little
longer
and re-imagined the things he saw
the white horses
the waiter
or the things he heard
about the accident
the story of the apple

the empty room echoes
to memory's footfall

switching off the light
is another ending
and he wonders
whether he will ever be as enchanted
as he once was

assuming that is what he felt

darkness smuggles
the pattern in the wallpaper
to somewhere else
somewhere beyond the lake
and the whispering wind

and he tries to recall it
the pattern
regular   rhythmical
woven into the fabric of his life
warp and weft
in and out

then an elsewhere voice

bring me some water would you?

and the empty promise of tomorrow
looms invisibly before him

fifteen fourteen thirteen

X

swap duvets with the weather
always too light
(or too heavy)
just right only that first time
the time you snuggle down
too comfortable to read
cocooned in harvested down
wrapped in the warp and weft of cotton

is that cover new, dear?

pattern suggesting a kind of
scandinavian tartan
and though the lines are rightly degreed
there is something in the shade
neither ochre nor burgundy
which suggests travesty
or impersonation

perhaps something woven
from circus cast-offs would be better
gaudy but cheerful

and as you allow yourself
to be swallowed whole
you remember that visit to the big-top
when you had been a child

risking enchantment

or so much later
at the restaurant when you ordered

what was it

or those times the park flooded
more or less
the water lapping at the land
the path
the empty pitches
from where caravans had been removed
as if that would ever be enough
to save them

or those that owned them

on the bedside table
a clock ticks

twelve eleven ten

but it is less like a clock
than the count of a juggler
the beat of an antique drum
there is something irregular
in the regularity
a secret
hidden in the gaps
between the sounds
or in the motion of the second-hand
that fragment of pause
when everything seems possible

and impossible at the same time

and you are left with
nothing
but the space in-between

listen

nine eight seven

can you hear the not-sound

the heavy-laden pause
the pregnancy in the moment
unattended
the point   still
which is neither one thing nor the other
where the world might turn
this way or that

in such moments

sense without enchantment

the rain might not come
the flood not happen
the car might not skid
the waiters remain resting on their elbows at
the counter

you might not have to choose
between ribollita and whatever else it was
or argue about the flood gauge
the colours of tartan
the heaviness of the duvet

six   five

but slip
instead
to sleep
or into autumn
or beyond autumn

is it cold, sir?

colder than you could ever know
beyond the compensation of duvets
or tea

milk first! milk first!

untouched by the antics of clumsy clowns
unthreatened by the lion
undefeated by the juggler's
ability (or inability) to count

four   three

to see
what
just there
beyond   or in

night-time eyelids
the blood pulse of tartan
the weft and warp of veins

and just between the count

two

comes that point
that still moment
when

time is withdrawn

and the antique drum stops
and the world pivots
and the answer is almost there

one

crash

Acknowledgements

The small quotes from the poetry of T.S.Eliot are taken from *Collected Poems, 1909-1962* by T.S.Eliot, Faber and Faber (1963).

Quotes are also taken from *Selected Poems: 1976-2022* by Ian Gouge, Coverstory books (2022).

www.ingramcontent.com/pod-product-compliance
Lightning Source LLC
Chambersburg PA
CBHW021124080526
44587CB00010B/639